W9-CRS-632

DATE DUE

Animal Lives

THE LIFE OF A RABBIT

By Jan Feder
Illustrated by Tilman Michalski

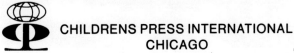
CHILDRENS PRESS INTERNATIONAL
CHICAGO

Library of Congress Cataloging in Publication Data

Feder, Jan.
  The life of a rabbit.

  (Animal lives)
  Translation of: Das Kaninchen.
  Summary: An account of a year in the life
of a wild rabbit and his family, followed by
text and illustrations presenting the physical
characteristics and behavior of rabbits.
  1. Rabbits—Juvenile literature. 2. Hares—
Juvenile literature. [1. Rabbits. 2. Rabbits—
Fiction] I. Michalski, Tilman, ill. II. Title.
III. Series.
QL737.L32F413 1982   599.32′2   82-9750
ISBN 0-516-08934-X   AACR2

North American 1982 Edition published
by Regensteiner Publishing Enterprises, Inc.

This evening Buck was farther from home than usual. His burrow was on the edge of the wood, but the fresh spring grass was much better here.

Suddenly he pricked up his ears. He got up on his hind legs and looked around, nervously. He sensed danger.

Buck was right. A hunter was coming. He had a dog with him. They were still a long way off, but Buck's sharp ears caught their faint sounds.

Better safe than sorry, thought Buck. He set off for home. Suddenly the dog barked—he had picked up Buck's scent.

Run! Only Buck's speed could save him now. He was almost flying but he couldn't keep it up for long.

Buck could hear the dog panting behind him. He could almost feel its hot breath on his back.

Nearly home, now. Buck zigzagged once more. With a final burst of speed he shot into his rabbit hole, exhausted.

The dog's angry barking echoed through the woods. All the rabbits had taken cover in their own burrows. At last the dog left, disappointed.

Buck had landed almost on top of his doe. He was too tired, and too scared, to move. But gradually the familiar smells of his home calmed him.

With the danger past, one rabbit after another came out into the evening light. But they stayed close to their burrows. They did not usually go far, even in the twilight when they felt safest.

Some of the rabbits grazed peacefully, and Buck's doe cleaned her back paws. But Buck was still nervous. He kept rising up on his hind legs to look around, sniff the air, and listen, making sure everything was safe.

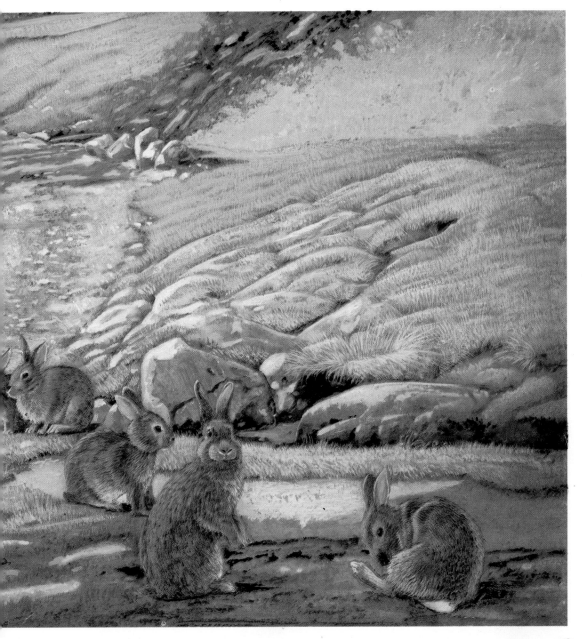

The strongest of the rabbits was leader of the colony. He went around each evening, checking that all was well. The other males kept out of his way.

One day Buck challenged him to battle. The two rabbits fought each other with their forepaws. But the leader was stronger and Buck lost the fight.

Springtime was mating time, and Buck was full of high spirits. He showed off for his doe, leaping into the air. Together they raced through the woods and fields. If a rival male appeared, Buck attacked at once, but he was nice to his doe.

A short time before the young were born, the doe dug a nursery burrow. It was away from the rest of the burrows. She lined it with grass and fur.

The babies were born hairless, blind, and deaf. Within a week they could see, hear, and crawl around, and their fur had grown.

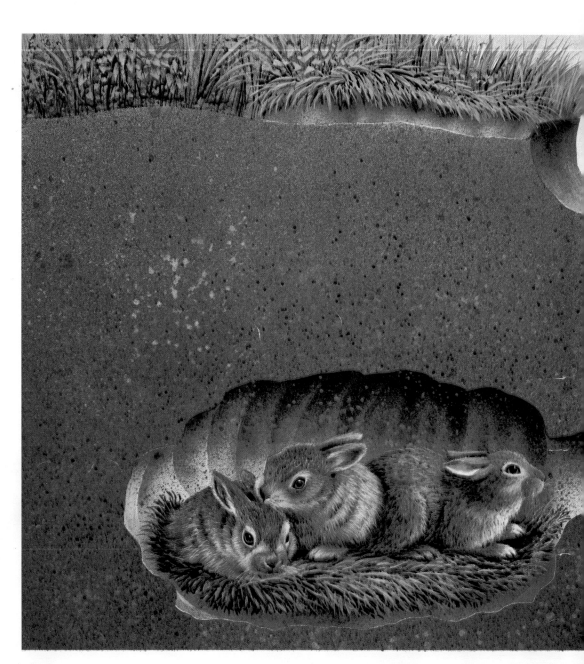

The doe did not stay with her babies. She came to the burrow to feed them, once or twice a day, usually at night. When she left, she carefully scratched earth over the entrance so that weasels and other predators would not find it.

One evening the doe peered cautiously out of her burrow. It was time to go and feed the babies. She did not sense any danger. She did not see the owl, sitting quite still in a tree. But the owl saw her.

It flapped its wings, rising from its perch to swoop down on the doe, silent and deadly.

Just in time the doe heard another rabbit thumping the ground in warning. Like a flash she doubled back and sped into her burrow. A narrow escape!

Three weeks passed. Now the young were almost grown. The doe fed them outside the burrow now, thumping her feet on the ground to tell them when she arrived. She kept watch while they played in the open. But she no longer covered the entrance when she left.

The doe was already expecting her next litter. Her first litter was on its own. The young males moved in with females living alone in burrows. The young females dug burrows for themselves. They waited for males to come and join them.

Buck and his doe had several litters during that year. Then came winter. Food became scarce. Buck sometimes went right up to houses. He ate bark from young trees and bushes, so that he could live until the spring came.

The Rabbit

A relative of the hare

For a long time hares and rabbits were thought of as rodents, but in fact they belong to a separate order of animals. Its scientific name is Lagomorpha. They are different from rodents in many ways. For instance, their teeth: hares and rabbits have *two* pairs of upper incisors, one behind the other. The composition of their blood is different from that of rodents, too. Unlike rodents they never use their forepaws for grasping objects, only for digging and for hitting things. Hares and rabbits are often seen stretching themselves, like cats. You will never see rodents,like rats or mice, stretching.

Rabbits can be found in North America, Europe, Africa, and other parts of the world. European rabbits are the domesticated rabbits in America. Wild rabbits in North America are called cottontails. Their tails are covered with soft, fluffy fur. When hopping, their tail looks like a bouncing, white ball.

Hares and rabbits are often mistaken for each other, because they live in the same kind of place, preferring fields and meadows, or the outskirts of woods. However, the wild rabbit is much smaller than the hare, and has shorter ears. Its coat is grayish, whereas the coat of the brown hare, as its name tells us, is brown or reddish brown. And while the rabbit's forelegs and hind legs are the same length, the hare's forelegs are much longer than its hind legs. So its head and chest are set higher than its rear end. There are two more ways of telling the hare and the rabbit apart. The hare is a solitary animal living above the ground, and making its nest or "form" in thick grass. The rabbit lives in a colony inhabiting a warren, which is a large system of burrows dug underground. Hares and rabbits usually keep out of each other's way.

Rabbit colonies

No one rabbit colony is exactly like any other in the number of its burrows and the way the burrows are laid out. However, every colony is ruled by a strong, experienced male or "buck," usually a fairly old rabbit, who is king of the colony. He lives in a large burrow in the middle of the warren. But the female rabbits, or "does," are in charge of dividing the colony into separate territories. They do the digging of the burrows. They dig with their front paws, scraping the loose earth away with their hind paws. Each doe settles in a particular part of the warren and considers it her home. She seldom moves more than a hundred meters away from it. She will defend it against other females. Young does usually dig their own burrows on the outer edges of the colony, so that the colony grows larger with each new litter.

The rabbit "king" looks over his kingdom every evening, to make sure that all is in order. The other males of the colony respectfully avoid him at that time. Sometimes, however, another buck will challenge the king. If the ruling rabbit loses the fight, the winner takes his place, inheriting his burrow and even his doe. There is an order of rank among the does, too. If the queen rabbit dies, another doe simply takes her place, and the rest of the females go on living in their own territories.

The mating of rabbits

Each male in a colony looks for a female and then moves into her burrow. We do not know for certain whether rabbit couples really stay together for a long time. But while the doe keeps to her own burrow, the buck will sometimes leave her and move in with another female.

How rabbits reproduce

We say of people with enormous families that they "breed like rabbits" because rabbits produce so many young. A doe rabbit's pregnancy lasts only a month. The mating season is from early spring to late summer. So a female can often have six litters a year, bearing up to thirty babies in all.

The Rabbit and its Body

The Skeleton

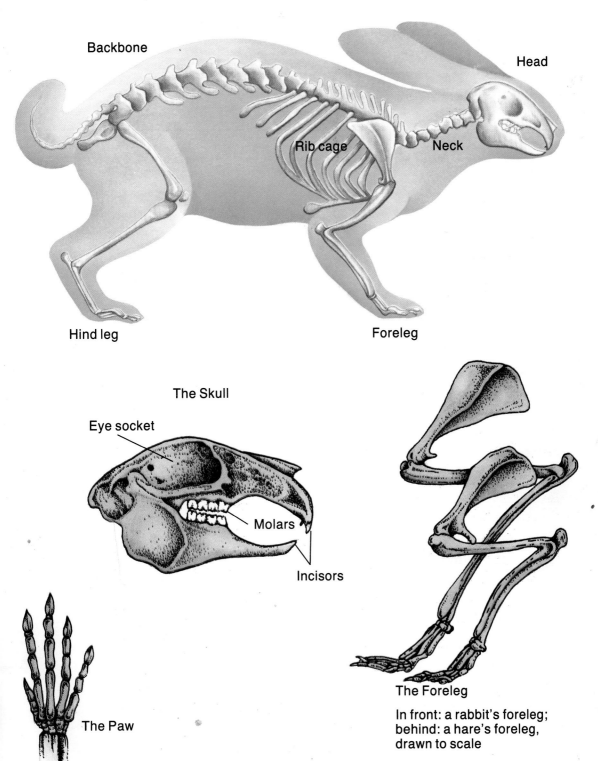

Backbone

Head

Rib cage

Neck

Hind leg

Foreleg

The Skull

Eye socket

Molars

Incisors

The Paw

The Foreleg

In front: a rabbit's foreleg;
behind: a hare's foreleg,
drawn to scale

A short time before the babies are born, the doe digs a nursery burrow in which they can nest. It is a plain hole, 1 to 3.2 yards (1 to 3 meters) long, broadening out into a hollow at the far end. She has her babies here. To protect them from beasts of prey, and indeed from her own rabbit relations, she usually digs the nursery burrow at least 109 yards (100 meters) away from the colony. She also scratches earth over the entrance to the burrow every time she visits it.

The doe suckles her young only once or twice a day. Usually she does not visit them to feed them until she can get there under cover of darkness. She spends the rest of the time back in her own burrow. As does usually become pregnant again as soon as the babies are born, her young can stay with her for only a month.

The babies are born hairless, blind, and deaf. They can soon hear, and their eyes open in about ten days. By the time they are a week old, they have grown fur. At first the mother suckles her young inside the burrow, and later on outside it. When the time comes she drives them away. Then the young bucks look for does with burrows of their own. The young does dig themselves burrows and wait for bucks to come and join them.

Habitat, food, and enemies of the rabbit

The European rabbit originally came from Spain, and was introduced to other Mediterranean countries by the Romans. Today, it is found all over Europe. It likes to dig its burrows in sandy, crumbly soil, choosing a place that offers some protection, such as the foot of a hill or the outskirts of a wood. Rabbits are often found living in pine woods.

Rabbits feed mostly at dawn. They are herbivorous animals, eating clover, grass, heather, and indeed almost all plants that grow wild in the meadows or are grown in fields as crops. Seven rabbits eat about as much as a fully grown sheep. So they can become a real pest to farmers, who may find they are losing a large part of the crops they grow. Rabbits have been a particular plague in Australia. They reproduced in enormous

The Rabbit and its Burrow

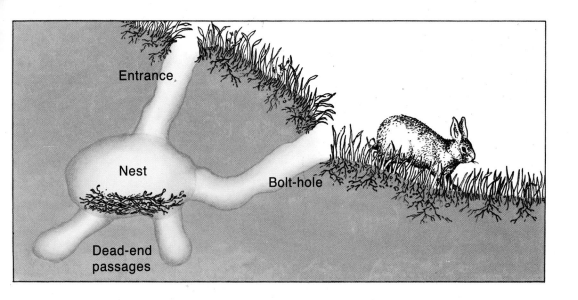

How the Rabbit Moves

Tracks left by a rabbit hopping slowly

Tracks left by a rabbit hopping fast

The Rabbit and its Relatives
(Lagomorpha)

Snowshoe rabbit (an American hare)

Pygmy rabbit

Bristly rabbit

Mexican Volcano rabbit

Brown hare

Antelope hare

Cape hare

Cottontail (the rabbit of the New World)

Blue, Alpine or mountain hare

Woolly hare

Red rock hare

Riu-Kiu rabbit

numbers after they were imported from England. Among the plants rabbits like best are grain crops and the tops of beets and potatoes. In autumn they will even dig up potatoes to eat them. In winter they eat the outer and inner bark of trees and bushes, doing a great deal of damage.

As well as ordinary excreta, rabbits produce small mucus-covered pellets of half-digested food which they swallow again. In this way they absorb as much nutrition from their food as possible.

The wild rabbit's natural enemies are foxes, weasels, stoats, buzzards, ravens, hawks, and owls. All these creatures help to keep down the number of rabbits. Man also tries to keep the rabbit population under control. Their natural life span is about nine years.

Behavior and sensory perception of the rabbit

The rabbit has two ways of moving. It hops, as shown on page 23. It can also slide along the ground, crouching down on its hind legs and hauling itself forward with its forelegs. You can see this movement when the rabbit is feeding, if it wants to get closer to stems, leaves, or blades of grass. However, hopping is its usual way of moving about.

Rabbits can move fast when they are in danger. But they cannot keep it up for long. So they seldom go very far from their burrows. If wild rabbits are caught and then set free more than 650 yards (600 meters) from their own colony, they do not find their way back. They settle where they were left.

A rabbit's senses of sight, smell, and hearing warn it of danger. If it wants to come out of its burrow, or graze peacefully in a meadow, it starts by making sure that the coast is clear. It will stop to look around, sniff the air, and listen for anything suspicious. The rabbit rears up to do this, either on its thighs or haunches. Or it stands right up on its hind legs. It can take in more information in this upright position. The rabbit's eyesight is not very good. If something moves, then a rabbit will notice the movement at once. But if an animal or human keeps perfectly still (and if the wind is not blowing in the rabbit's direction) the rabbit may not actually see the danger. It

The Rabbit and its Body Language

Washing

Resting

Stretching

On the alert

Digging

Alarm

may even run straight toward it. As if to make up for its poor eyesight, the rabbit's eyes are set on the sides of its head, so that it has a larger field of vision. Rabbits can even see things moving behind their backs.

The rabbit's sense of smell is better developed. Rabbits point their noses into the wind, to pick up scents better. If the weather is unfavorable for picking up scents, they are at a disadvantage. However, the rabbit can always rely on its sense of hearing. Its big, almost trumpet-shaped ears can be turned in all directions. They pick up the slightest sound.

The tame rabbit

When the Romans found wild rabbits in Spain, they soon realized that they were a useful source of food. So they kept hares and rabbits in big enclosures. In the same way the people of the Middle Ages kept rabbits on a large scale in enclosed warrens.

We do not know just when wild rabbits began to be tamed and bred as domestic animals. But it is thought that the French monks of the Middle Ages were the first to keep rabbits as pets. The tame rabbit's senses are not nearly as sharp as those of a wild rabbit. But many new and often beautiful varieties of tame rabbit have been reared by breeding (some are shown on page 29). Many of these varieties deserve to be called pedigree rabbits.

Besides providing us with meat, rabbits give us fur for coats. And the Angora rabbit gives us knitting wool.

Some Breeds of Tame Rabbit

Belgian Hare (really a rabbit)

Netherlands Dwarf

Harlequin

English Lop-ear

Angora

Blue Vienna

Interesting Facts about Rabbits

Rabbit Land

About three thousand years ago the Phoenicians landed on the Iberian peninsula. They found there an animal that reminded them of the hyrax, or rock rabbit, which lived in their own country (the "coney" referred to in the Bible). In their Semitic language the word for hyrax was "Shaphan." So the Phoenicians called the land they had just discovered "I-shepan-im," meaning "Island of the Rock Rabbits." (Actually what they had found was the ancestor of the European wild rabbit.) In Latin "I-shepan-im" became "Hispania," *i.e.* Spain. So Spain, still considered the rabbit's country of origin, really means Rabbit Land.

The name of the rabbit

Our word "rabbit " may come to us by way of Old French. There is a related French dialect word for rabbit, "rabotte," and the Walloon dialect of French spoken in Belgium has the word "robete." The Dutch for rabbit is "robbeken." In several languages the word for a rabbit comes from the Latin word "cuniculus." The Italian word is "coniglio," the German "kaninchen," and the Danish "kanin."

Keeping rabbits under control

Keeping down the number of rabbits is always a problem. Traditionally, farmers and gamekeepers have kept them under control by trapping or shooting them. Their natural enemies such as stoats, weasels, and birds of prey help the farmer too. In the 1950s, when the large number of rabbits had become a real problem to farmers, the disease of *myxamotosis* was introduced to the countries of Western Europe, and wiped out a large part of the rabbit population. *Myxamotosis* is fatal only to rabbits of the Old World (including those in Australia, which were taken there

from England), but they are now becoming immune to it. It is quite a mild disease for the rabbits of the New World.

Improvised burrows

Rabbits cannot always choose an ideal place to dig their burrows, but they are inventive. In areas that flood, they have been found living in hollow trees. Rabbit les have been found under stacks of ood and railway lines, in sewers and ainpipes, and under the floors of huts at have no underground foundations. ey will even invade cemeteries and dig rrows under the gravestones.

bbits as laboratory animals
abbits make useful laboratory animals r scientists, particularly for medical ientists who are doing research into w ways of curing people, and who need experiment on live creatures.

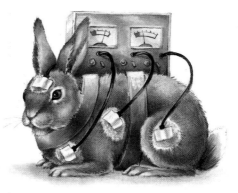

undreds of thousands of rabbits are ed in laboratories as experimental imals every year. (Many people object using live animals for this kind of search.)

bbits that steal milk
veryone knows that rabbits are a pest to rmers because they destroy crops. ometimes they have even been seen ilking goats. A milkmaid once found a bbit sucking the udder of a goat who as thought to have run dry some time fore—no wonder, since the rabbit had ready been at her udder before the aid came to milk her.

Rabbits and hares in our language and literature
There are many sayings about hares in the English language. We say someone is "harebrained" if he acts wildly and rashly. Or perhaps we might say he is "mad as a March hare." Both these phrases refer to the wild way hares act during their springtime mating season. Our only proverbial expression to do with rabbits, "breeding like rabbits," refers to all the young they produce. However, rabbits appear often in literature: there are Beatrix Potter's Peter Rabbit and the Flopsy Bunnies, and Benjamin Bunny; Lewis Carroll's White Rabbit in *Alice in Wonderland;* Br'er Rabbit in Joel Chandler Harris's *Uncle Remus* stories; and Richard Adams's popular story about wild rabbits, *Watership Down.*

One sweater a year
An Angora rabbit gives about 14 ounces (400 grams) of wool a year—enough to knit a child's sweater.

Index